*The Cape Breton
Book of the Dead*

The Cape Breton
Book of the Dead

Don Domanski

Anansi Toronto

© Don Domanski 1975

House of Anansi Press Limited
35 Britain Street
Toronto, Canada M5A 1R7

Designed and produced in Canada
by the Coach House Press.
Photo by Paul Harris.

Published with the assistance of the Canada Council
and the Ontario Arts Council.

ISBN 0-88784-135-X   HAP 34

Canadian Shared Cataloguing in Publication Data

Domanski, Don.
    The Cape Breton Book of the Dead.

(House of Anansi poetry series; HAP 34)
ISBN 0-88784-135-X

I. Title.

PS8557.04C3   811'.5'4
PR9199.3.D

for Mary

Contents

Tenement   11
Childhood Memory   12
Old Women   13
Visitors   14
The Widower   15
Beldam   16
Geraniums   17
Cactus   18
The Cape Breton Book of the Dead   19
Deserted Farmhouse   20
Stone   21
Gossip   22
Finch   23
Vulcan Avenue   24
The Beaten Hound   25
Flea   26
Scavenger   27
American Tourists   28
Citizen   29
Remaining Fragment of a Lecture by a Professor   30
A Creation   31
Cat   32
Parkmothers   33
Portrait   34

Accident   35
The Arrest   36
Summer Job: Hospital Morgue   37
Vancouver   38
Necropolis   39
Today All Killing   40
Edge   41
To a Boy Lost in the Forest and Believed Dead   42
Flies   43
Toads   44
Frog   45
The Wolf's City   46
Cat Burial in English Bay   47
Witchsketch   48
Madonna   49
Wife Cleans House   50
Three Notes Toward a Love Poem   51
The Beginning   52
Amabael   53
Angels   54
Rebirth   55
Constellation   56
Astronaut   57
Prophet   58
Nightwalk   59

Tenement
   (to my parents)

here Lucifer
wears the beaten child in his hair

watches this stratus of buildings
drift gently out each night
past earthlight
toward the wide art of stars

only to be hauled back each morning
by City Council
the Mayor tugging the huge tow rope.

Childhood Memory

my mother cracked open
a family story
and the tea was poured again.

while all along
the hills of the moon
I heard the tale retold

I heard the distance claim it
and saw us all fall dead.

Old Women

not unlike mice
they gather between the walls
to curse the trap

and marvel at the house plant.

only the wedding ring or the coffin
bring them together like this
to share a darkening room

only those two objects
flush them out of the tall grass
where they hide (downed starlings)
from the rock and the tom cat.

Visitors

these are Lucifer's fingers
five of them
puffy-white
sticking out of the floor
each posing as a man
each telling me
they're only here to help.

fingerprints
burn into me
from across the room.

already I'm out of control.

this is Satan's hand
moving towards me
through the doorway.

The Widower

sixty years to jollify
an otherwise forbidding face

now a little coin of a man
round and polished (her expenditure)

with well behaved affinities
he dances nightly in his room
not forgetting to toast her health

to rib her presence into laughter.

Beldam

old phoenix you rise
out of morning tea

out of a single cup
left by itself on the kitchen table

old gal, old wart, your celtic pounds
simply balance the house when it teeters
your remedies never cure
your advice is always wrong
your kindness drowns cats
and overwaters the geranium

old grandmother, old sister, old wife,
old sweetheart, old heart in pre-War condition
what carries your soft body
to breakfast?

what sly tongue has chatted your head awake?

Geraniums

massive tempers
shaking their roots and displacing a tom's howl
with their own sudden cry
from the windowsill

all day trembling for light and water
yet at times rejoicing in tribal amazement
at their particular luck with living

when night comes I lie down with them
not as lover but to awake rooted
to become a wildman in a geranium pot
a recluse ten years gone.

Cactus

spikes still aimed
in an ancient pose
against the earth
it sits on my living room table

a war monument

a sutra that explains how a man
must protect himself from the world

it dreams of nothing but water
sees nothing but desert
fills the room with its one stubborn head.

The Cape Breton Book of the Dead
(for Mark and Judy Johnstone)

still a solid citizen
a worthy guy dreaming

still an answerable head
filled with pibroch
lined with stones that once carried him
to the coal-shed door

in all his eighty years
while undercover in this district
his strength grew
mythical in his dialect

yet now if he coaxes his end
he'll strain the family likeness
(the labour of a joke
and the ancestral laughter)

if even he forgets the angels
(bigger than a shithouse they are)
he'll lose his way
between the wallpaper and the stars.

Deserted Farmhouse
(Coxheath Cape Breton)

after the meltage of years nothing stands
but a half-chair and solid roof
for a dead Mrs.

nothing but her tonnage
her absolute ownership
of the few floorboards
and remaining light

the bent fork in the corner
once handled every day
is now a door

these nails and beams
are also her occult
her way back

looking beyond my face
she views a different yard
with smaller trees
and someone doing something
very ordinary and exciting.

Stone
(for Bessie)

that is your stone.

you are now somehow important
an axis in a small world
that for a time will turn on your memory

and when it is evening
and they gather in a room
only a photograph or a chair
or a favorite window
will set them talking

and they will pass the stone
from person to person
and speak all the sentences for you.

that is your stone
heavy and pale
like your last face.

Gossip

my neighbour's cooing can lax the moment
can ease this room's situation

her eyes likewise hang on out of kindness
(balancing them in the eaves)

true-blue is accomplished every morning
(raising Junior and Miss to an effective beginning)
by managing the far off streets
and the record-smashing return with food.

Finch

a skit of feather and bone

an old weight
skimming the yard
with an eye
for tabby
and house-drudge

above the coal shed
the twist of theorem in mid-flight

no demon
surely not Lucifer
yet in the quick climb
a true competitor for Man.

Vulcan Avenue

under the street light
the corner boys are ousting every laugh from zero

they are the miracles
or if not the miracles of these streets
they are simply their own solid heads
squared against disaster

they come after the inane underfoot of pavement
to discuss their possibilities
and the world's end

on their arms they've made crude tattooes
with sewing needles and ink.

The Beaten Hound

the torpor of chain and dish
is a man with a stick
to beat to submission a dog and a oneupmanship of stars
over a kennel

is a circulatory system hung from a brain
as a red banner of power
to fathom the excitable eyes
and elegant snout with a cry for obedience

nothing will save the decorum of fleas and hunger
from a someday fatal clubbing
from a final frostwork on spilt blood

it will be done
(already a dream emerges of digging a grave
for the getup of death).

Flea

this ticking child
with all its eyes opened
with all its legs held
between my fingertips
this blood relative
found on my leg
what can I do with you?
I don't believe
in even small executions
but what's to be done?
I can't talk you out of it
can't change your mind
you're nature's boy
you know what tastes good
what makes you drunk and happy.

I dig my fingernail
into its neck
its head drops
a thousand miles
to the floor.

Scavenger

the debonair gleam
of blood
on the torn finger

the sacrificial ash
in pores of cheek and hand

this earth's centre
beneath a work-shirt
sweats and breathes in
the smell of burning rubbish

breathes in the ether
of rotting fruit and decaying flesh

supports his family
with a quick hand in the fire
to bring out a piece of clothing
a box of pies
a half gone world still eatable
still useable
still better than any other.

American Tourists

coming across the Disney border
Minnie the Mouse and Mickey
packed for skiing in July
wearing buttons that say
I AM A TOURIST.

hunting Halifax for Eskimos

although I was mean
I become sentimental
imagining them now
in Newark New Jersey
in Kansas City
and Santa Fe

back home with slides
and back scratchers
that read simply
CANADA.

Citizen

at work he dreams
of bolts and bed clothes
at the other end of the city

at home he dreams
of a spider's leg
kicking over the office blocks

sex and money break his heart
drain his belly

his back is a lectern

for the world
that teaches him manners.

Remaining Fragment of a Lecture by a Professor

boys and girls
I'm here to tell you
that the only real face I have
is one dog-eared in a copy
of *Boys Annual*
left in my very first desk
(one similar to yours
but much much smaller)
and that I've had many desks since

and sometimes at night
they all appear
metal ones and wooden ones
clanking into my bedroom
helping themselves
leaving bolts and splinters
on my wife's body when they're through...

A Creation

the executive
is the mosquito's figment

the pen set
the moist hand shake
the enthusiasm for golf
were products of free time
enveloped in hot static air
over the pond's surface

goaded along the tips of mare's tail
the loud tie
and secretary's body
fell into place

proverbs such as:
"If I don't someone else will"
and "I didn't make the rules"
came later.

Cat
(for Lü)

1
your body and mind
are death sentences
in unison.

2
this morning on my bed
you've left me
your final statement on everything

its face dried red
its stomach completely gone.

3
you are the Buddha
blood stained
with a perfect conscience.

Parkmothers

in the park
mothers stop
to feed their children trees and grass

to smell the pigeons
and to laugh

to open their purse
to close their legs
to chew their nails
to scratch their bites

to contemplate
their openings.

Portrait

in the dog's mouth
the cat is shaken
to a dead stereotype

above them along Tupper street
the moon and tenements soft-shoe
for comedy relief.

Accident

after the fifty year placing of props
this is death's rehearsal

the gist of brain
awakening among the midden of metal
and glass

the split bone
the freetrade of blood.

The Arrest
  (a Christmas carol for Barbara Purdy)

the police caught up with us
and there beneath their hands
on the snow covered parking lot
we became mute pliable roses
for their wives

basketballs for their sons
pop-records for their daughters
colour TV for the whole family

Christmas presents
finally piled high in the back seat
of the patrol car.

Summer Job: Hospital Morgue

smug and exhausted
each lay like a satisfied craftsman

each a heroism looming
in front of me still

some only heads in bags
some about to spring to their feet
bursting with laughter at the joke

by midsummer their shattered bodies
and bad timing were commonplace
almost forgettable

now years later I remember detail
a half painted nail   a half opened eye
a clenched fist

a brief heart to heart with an irredeemable face.

Vancouver

looking across English Bay
I thought of the wolf and amoeba
once hunting Grouse Mountain
of parking lots creeping into orbit
of a patrol car blowing out the stars

I waited for a department store's mindless energy
to wake its caricatures
the expanse of citizens
(the monstrous form of a floorwalker
asleep on his pillow).

Necropolis

the rat's stomach is opened to the stars
a nebula placed in its bowel

rat face
and rat hide wait
in the city that grows like a rat's dream might
if rat knew algebra and alphabet

and had control of ballpoint
and pad

waits on the doorstep
for a rat's burial
in trash can or fire.

no one in that dark house
is now thinking about four rat paws
hardening on painted wood

no one expects to step on a necropolis
in the morning.

Today All Killing

today all killing happens in this body
beneath this flesh:

the man hunted down in his room
the shark swimming into its meat
the moth boiling in the spider's brain
the sparrow flying a worm to the roof

tired and cold
each death stops here to rest
to lay down its cracked head and dream.

Edge

I've come to the edge of a forest
that is capable of anything

wolves will not enter
but become ground beetles
and leave

this place is a turning point

the forest has lips and eyes
and rivers

they all stop and wait

beneath me
worms turn the earth
on its axis.

To a Boy Lost in the Forest
and Believed Dead
(his body never having been found)

your body is no longer your own
the catbird has it
and the fox
each holds an end
and moves swiftly away from the other

your body doesn't snap
it stretches
it yawns flesh from ground
to sky

it moves through the countryside
a thin pink world
which no one sees.

Flies

they arrive with a talent like men
for living
for carrying their purpose to its extreme

claiming these rooms
as they would spoiled food or a corpse
they expand their evangelism

locked into sermons
willing to give advice
but not to accept

they are always pioneers
Puritans escaping suppression
having landed here
not to compromise
but to establish themselves

I am a man staring out in wonder
between trees

I am their Indian.

Toads

such little bags of dirt
minding their own business

out of a hag's recipe
to stare blankly
across gravelled road
through exhaust fumes
over the rising dust
and flattened bodies of toads

patient and vacant
like miniature shopgirls
their minds elsewhere:

Orion spinning
with psalms
or
the earth's centre bulging
with their one thought.

Frog

the pond's mongrel

yet no mere brute
could bark the land into night
and love intensely such wives

no mere mutt
could sit lunged and complacent
among the duckweed

with a tail wagging elsewhere.

The Wolf's City

is himself.

where all buildings have smells
and noses to smell back

where all the crowds rush about
to buy one thing
then devour it immediately

where the musk of elk and caribou
drifts down every night covering the roofs of cars
and high-rises.

is a place where no one
is
but him

where all entrances
are erased each night
by the rubbing of a snout.

Cat Burial in English Bay
   (for Igor)

the night air comforts

yet the head crushed beneath the wheel
still has its appetite for vanity

yet the fundamental victim
weighs the sack
through to the earth's core

this is someone's word
about to be spoken

someone's hierarchy
about to gain power.

Witchsketch

a lady's privacy:

        (1) dead primrose
        (2) knobs of her face
        (3) moil of a perfect day

a few concerns:

        (A) stuffing Matthew Hopkins heaven
            stomach with pizzles and hobs
        (B) overriding science
        (C) holding up her boil to moonlight

a footnote:

        she's sullen with owlets
        still throned in the New World
        Queenly over Europe

Madonna

springtails found her
in the morning

with a belly full of water
and a lunar face
among the frogbit.

there was no prophecy.

she merely came
with the downpour
to bless the backswimmers
and the water shrew

and although for days after
did not labour
to bring forth child-god
or word
was loved

by the busy populace

the single water flea
that clung faithfully to her lips
her head knocking against the shore.

Wife Cleans House
 (to Toni Guy)

wife crawls beneath rocks
and comes out with salamanders
and beetles in her dust pan

wife places her hands in a pond
and brings up the bottom
in a plastic bag

wife climbs to the tops of trees
and throws starlings to the ground
then sweeps them away

wife plants seeds
and lamps appear
and mahogany tables
and a chesterfield
and quiet pictures
of the family.

Three Notes Toward a Love Poem

(1) the full blast of Autumn
     along the ground.

(2) a few birches alone
     among them a man thinking.

(3) enter a moon and someone
     standing at the other end of the field
     with a cigarette and a word in her mouth

     both glowing red.

The Beginning
   (Feb. 1969)

he awoke and believed himself heirloom
to her speech and flesh
far more than an upstart to her full form

and so foraging through he arrived
finally at her door as an accomplished stone or leaf
to landmark her every word
to expand her every laugh

to recuperate beneath the exchange of hours
(their slow process of shouldering the landscape
between them).

Amabael
(Angel of Winter)

whose pigment am I
that I do not blush
at my winning ways

at my ease with everything?

whose possessions do I tend?
(rolling them over and over in their sleep
ransacking their belly
cracking their bone)

whose eternity?
whose dominion?

taking a breath
I devil the air with snow
to double my immensity.

Angels

balanced like gulls
above the relapse of sea and rock
their heads slowly turn
a complete twist toward land

they carry burning swords and pen-names
like Michael and Israfel
but know themselves as larvae
twirling in a man's ear
or a rat gnawing away at a wall

dead Heaven's moil
they now drift spore-like toward anyone's mind
their silence thumping loudly
on the boulders drowning the water's edge

the Big Dipper rising
to bare its incisors over the sea.

Rebirth

stunned by the comeback
each person met
spewed out their luckless arguments

weightless
her name rose drumming its chest
above the house

from a room walked in all winter
she had risen up complete (an effective mandate)
legendary above the floorboards.

Constellation

spring
and the Small Dog is staring at the horizon

he has given up looking
for escape or a bitch
or a solid white bone
to hold between his teeth

his god spins him
by the tail
forcing out each bark
that spreads across the sky
falling finally
upon the city
to become solid things:
axe blades
and the fists of young men.

Astronaut

with half a mind for Orion
and half a mind for Gemini
I plan a path through a universe
of Mythologies and Dogs.

outside, the unkillable blackness
of God's one pupil
expands.

I sit back and watch it all
the legend of myself unfolding
with the pressing of buttons.

Prophet

I'm a prize

a good habit

some words between God
and Man

when He aimed His eye
at mountains and villages
and was about to

I was born
a safety valve

at once I began to pray
to sing Him asleep
among his Commandments.

Nightwalk

this night splayed from my head
is gossamer and cool

a dog-genius walks with me
points out the optical owls
fetches the stick flung at Taurus

around us without abandon
the combines of tree and rock
stand dazed in their own enlightenment

never witness our path
or hear
the dog call everything
by its proper name.

198285

Some of these poems have appeared in *Canadian Forum*, *The Dalhousie Review*, *Fiddlehead*, *Northern Light*, *Prism International*, *Quarry*, and *Storm Warning II*.

The author wishes to thank the Ontario Arts Council for its assistance.

DATE DUE

GAYLORD			PRINTED IN U.S.A